Rivering

Kimberly L. Becker

I0560739

SPUYTEN DUYVIL

New York City

Acknowledgments:

Blue Hole Spring:
  Indigenous Message on Water, Volume II
Rivering, Skin Stories, What This Ceremony is Not:
  South Dakota Review
Rivering reprinted and featured:
  Poetry Daily
The Opposite of Ichthus:
  Under A Warm Green Linden, Indigenous Ecopoetry Issue
Headwaters, Eagle Blessing (as Migration), Tributary, Water Cycle:
  Anglican Theological Review

Thank you to Barbara Duncan for translating "Blue Hole Spring" into the
Cherokee language

With gratitude to Shawn Crowe for being so supportive of my work
and for friendship over many years

With appreciation to Spuyten Duyvil for welcoming this work

Robert F. Fox: wetAxkoosšteeRAt & tatasistA

Rivers flow in Kimberly L. Becker's poems. The words and images come together from a land of disappeared, drowned places in song like water, telling stories and singing songs of justice, reparation, remembrance and blood. Becker's voice resounds in the open places of these poems.

Jamie Parsley,
North Dakota Associate Poet Laureate, author of *Salt* and *Echo*

We are all drowning sometimes, sinking under the water, but with Kimberly Becker's Rivering we are reminded that we are also often looking up for the light. You'll find yourself reading through the occasionally murky water to understand the past but in a liminal way. Reading about both the river's, and into our own pasts, we can understand our futures. Looking closely can show us the river's own terrible historical beauty, and can also be transformative. There is love and longing in what results. We river along with Becker and feel her angst but also, importantly, the love. Don't forget to look up through the water. Maybe we haven't been sinking under but slowly floating up the whole time.

Chris Arvidson, author of *Nobody Cares What You Think*

Kimberly L. Becker's sixth poetry book flows with meaning and quiet emotion as she carries us along on her personal explorations and reflections regarding place, connection, language, love, and tribal history. "[T]he river is Indigenous, / sinuous, ingenious / Always flowing ..." This is a rich, moving read —insightful in depth and defiant in spirit.

Deborah Jang, author of *Float True* and *Last Will* and *Best Guesses*

for my son

Some time when the river is ice ask me/
mistakes I have made. Ask me whether/
what I have done is my life.
—William Stafford from "Ask Me"

You think you can return to that place
—Sherwin Bitsui from "Flood Song (extract)"

Contents

River Speak

I have many names:
Missouri, Big Muddy,
the Great Mystery
The last is my truest name,
my favorite name
But names try to pin down
and say they know me
whereas I am always changing
and moving
When they tried to trap me
I swirled in anger
I still flow under
the reservoir,
still push as much as I can
against the dam
I still contain life,
but I miss those
who lived along my banks
for so, so long
They belonged there
Together, we were home
My power is their power,
even living up above,
even living by the lake
they fashioned of my flow,
what was below was not washed away
It is still in my memory
still in their blood
Blood is mostly water

Our lives will never be separate
I never gave away my power
I can still destroy at will
My tears at being captured
cleansed and flowed onward
with the currents

Write/Right

What right have I to write these words?
This is not my history nor home,
but the Cherokee in me sees similarities
between this flood and our own:
Cherokee towns drowned
Graves buried under
water
Some blood memory
recognizes the same wrong
All there is, is this:
the desire to mark a loss
and seek reparations
for what never should have been
To name names
so this will never be forgotten,
not even when the elders
have ceased to tell their stories
These words will right nothing
These words will write something

WHILE YOU SLEPT

BirdCast offers live bird migration maps and tracking

While you slept,
　　　1,089,200 birds
flew over on migration
　　　　　　You read this and imagine
them having dipped their wings
　　　　　　　　into your dreams
the warblers and sparrows
　　　　　　　　at 1,200 feet
flying an average of 21 miles an hour
　　　　　　　　　　　No wonder you were restless:
the animal you sensing their movement
　　　　　　　　　　　　Driving at dawn one
　　　　　　　　　morning
you had watched in fascination
　　　　　　　　　　　　　as flocks of
　　　　　　　　　　unknown birds
kept creating murmuration after murmuration,
　　　　　　　　　　　　　　　mes-
　　　　　　　　　　　　　　merizing you
　　　　　　　　　　　　　　with kaleido-
　　　　　　　　　　　　　　scopic
changes
as the sun rose in splendored changelessness

FOLLOW

in honor of the Sahnish

I say we have Selu (Corn Mother), too
You say your tribe followed Mother Corn
up from the South,
farther and farther North
Some stayed behind
Some went farther North than you
You were led to a place
rich in all your needs
The Missouri bent
like an elbow
where trees gave cover
and soil was rich for growth
and there was plenty to hunt and fish
You were faithful to follow
There you lived in peace
You believed the worth
of the words of the treaty
you were mistaken to trust
You have followed Mother Corn
You continue to pray
and follow your old ways
even though your home
was flooded
even though you were displaced
to another place
You still know who you are
You still hold your reservoir of memories
Even after drowned towns,

your spirit rises above
You trust and honor Mother Corn
who gives you sustenance
when all else was taken, stolen

Eternal Flame

At Sequoyah's birthplace museum (near
where he was born, but actual
location was flooded by creation
of Tellico Lake) I walk to memorial,
common grave of those who lived and died in
Little Tennessee Valley prior to flooding
from Tellico Reservoir. I circle
to remember lives of those whose graves were
excavated before their remains
would have been buried under rising water
I circle to release and wish them peace
then walk farther to the waiting water
where I search for shells and find white spirals
that have lain in the silt as witnesses
I leave some shells on the edge of the mound in honor
of the dead and will take some back to the Northern
Plains where they will continue to whisper stories
of Tanasi and Chota, all underwater,
while at Blythe Ferry I visit memorial
of Cherokee forced onto the Trail of Tears
At Red Clay I walk dappled sunlit trail
to Blue Hole Spring where I offer prayers for
the Real People who still survive Removal
There in that peaceful place of healing, final
words come floating past like fallen leaves:
I am sorry that I am not strong enough
to have been what I should have been for you
Happiness is an unexpected gift
this late in life. The Eternal Flame was

not burning that day, but I could still see
the image of fire from within the stone
and still hear the rattle and warrior's cry
and still see the War Dance, welcome and warning

Sky

I watched
I sent scouts of clouds to observe
how they dug and scarred the earth
to create this concrete capturer
My rain of tears did not absolve them
My own small flood said: I am one with the river
I still see what others can't
I shapeshift from blue to white with snow
I send ice to thicken the surface
accruing even more layers to defy the auger
None of this augurs well
The river continues flowing under
what you wrought
while I still watch in witness
I saw a worker fall to his death
and my first thought was *he deserves it*
Then I remembered that Creator
will do the judging and avenging
Still, in howls of protest,
I send a calvary of wind
to sear and sting
until all is whiteout
whitewhitewhite
outoutout

DIPTYCH/DOUBLE VISION:

I. The Beauty of the Now

You don't see loss
You see where you played as a child
where you rode your horse into the water,
jumped off his back, swam under his legs
You knew; you'd heard stories of the flood,
but for you, it was always the lake
You say you know the history,
but don't dwell on it
Instead, you say you choose
to focus on the beauty of the now
I try to look at it that way,
but all I see is loss
The same way I saw it in Georgia,
North Carolina, Tennessee, where Cherokee
towns were drowned
We stand, looking out onto the water
You tell me to close my eyes and listen
to the river that still pushes forward,
despite the dam
Waves nudge the shore, saying
remember, remember
below our current beauty
runs the current of what
we knew before
before towns were
covered
before the bottomlands
of home
were drowned
down
and
down
and
down

II. Shimmer

Lake shimmers and nuzzles the shore
like a horse nuzzling your palm for feed
There you swam and rode your horses
into mirrored water
You'd heard stories of lost towns, the flood,
but for you it was a happy place
You say you appreciate the beauty of the now,
even though you know the past
You tell me this as we stand by a cemetery
where the dead chime in about how
the water rose right up to their bones
how the power contained is volatile
how the water's dreams spill over the banks
I look and see drowned towns,
just like in Tanasi
I am unable to focus on the surface
This is the difference between us
Yet I never swam there as a child,
never saw this lake as a joyful place
We stand and watch together,

separate in our vision

House from Below

The house is unassuming now,
but was grand then, when bishops
visited from as far away as Fargo
This house saw the land moving
beneath it as it was jacked up
and moved to higher ground

So many dislocations in life

I dream of our home place,
smoke rising from a long-cold chimney
To swim in this water would feel
like the chill of betrayal
This house still has life
after removal
We carry ourselves from home to home
Carrying memories, escaping the flood
that rises behind us
What holds?
Doorframe
Walls
Steps to front porch
Windows eyeing new life, new green,
but also watching for threat,
adapting to new location
Learned grandeur in transition
I climb the steps to sit on the porch
and watch for remembered changes

Headwaters

This strange land formed and haunted by movement of glaciers. Outsized rocks called cannonballs.

Remembering cannonball holes in brick in colonial Williamsburg. Remembering how the Thomas Legion fought for land already stolen. What starts, what forms, from where? You spread the family genogram out like a map (arbitrary lines imposed on ancestral lands) and see all the trauma lines

leading to you. You decide to break the secrecy, starting with your son. Some see only the present. Someone says in my presence *It's been a hundred years; they should get over it* Now Arctic glaciers are calving too often. Now the water is rising in Appalachia, on the Plains, interspersed with fire and drought. You come upon a washed-out road; have to decide whether to try to drive through it.

Decide against the risk of being washed away, but turning back is no better. You see the car filling with water, break the glass like you were ready to do on the Bay Bridge. Your sweat is cold; you begin to sink in syncope. You remember to take the next breath. You remember the source of your strength. You watch a crane lift off as bombers mark the airspace.

What this Ceremony is Not

       This ceremony is not for forgiveness
It is for chosen sacrifice
       This ceremony is not your altar
It belongs to us
There we place our prayers
Here we lift our prayers
There is no prayer book
These prayers are in our bones
       This ceremony is not for the dead
It is for the living
Cast out misplaced hope,
the shame and trauma
inherited by blood
What is it that you hold behind your back?
Offer that up, too
No room for falsehood here
       This ceremony is not an inversion
of good medicine
       This ceremony is not Christian,
that colonizing religion
       This ceremony is not for you
You took our home,
but you will never take our ways
       This ceremony is not for forgiveness

Skin Stories

Listen, these things cannot be known
unless shared and passed down
For some of us there are breaks
in the lineage, secrecy and shame
The jack rabbit is white in winter,
brown in summer
Adapt and assimilate
if it means survival
Your dark hair and skin,
mine light that burns at the beach
then peels away
When I take you home,
you stand by the waterfall
gushing from mountain,
surrounded by laurels
This flow
and the flow of my river,
running North
The red salamander
I found in the creek
as a kid
The threat of copperhead
and rattlesnake
My teacher saying to me
that we Cherokee respect how snakes can shed their skins
and become new snakes
These days follow on old days
White jack rabbit disappears into
canvas of snow

Copperhead retreats into rock wall
Later, I gather skeins of skins
left by blacksnakes in the basement
There's even one in the dryer
where they went for warmth

WHITEOUT

Snow
       sinuous
like sand
You strain to see the lines
Then without warning: whiteout
You become disoriented,
can't see anything but snow
You turn on hazards, slow
You can't tell where you are
Afraid to stop, afraid to forge ahead

Boundaries blur
There is no safe space
White lake, white land
All covered by storm
that—suddenly—clears
You can make out the road
You can inch your way home
Emergency kit unused in the back
Your hands hurt from gripping so tight

You think of history whited-out, covered over,
ignoring what was there, what will always be there
You look at your skin, perceived as white, despite
your undocumented heritage
Snow, sinuous like sand
takes you back, to the mountains,
to the Outer Banks
You remember reading that

white light contains all wavelengths of visible light
White is the sum of all possible colors
In that whiteout you quickly learned humility
You were awed by a power
over which you have no control
Snow shifts
      across the highway,
sinuous
      as sand
In summer, cottonwood tufts
      will blow like snow,
recalling winter's blizzards,
winter's hazards

FOUNDATION

from church in White Shield, ND brought up from below
then lost to fire; now part of a project of remembrance,
thanks to a grant for environmental reparations

Finally found
after we forged through high grass
carpeted with the silver of sacred sage
and there it is, staunchly standing

Brought up from below,
saved from flood,
it served until finally felled
by fire
Now its wound
is filled with cast-off
appliances and other junk

Still, its steps do not
lead to nowhere—
they ascend to cobalt sky,
witness to all the prayers
once held here,
all the old hymns
lifted into singing wind

We stand at the top of the steps,
you, inheritor, and I, interloper
We take a selfie to document our presence
Behind sunglasses, my eyes water with emotion

TRIBUTARY

Everything feeds into something else
We join and join
Missouri, Mississippi, Ohio, Tennessee
and all the lesser rivers
We flow and flow
Your tribe sets out reminders in the water
of your presence and evidence of new life
that will continue onward
in the flow of history,
in the stories of elders,
including the river
This system of water
Network of movement,
not stasis
Damming the power
for power of control
fails to regard the floodplains' need of regular
natural flood, so life can thrive
Dams on the upper made the lower worse
Deluge of memories not contained
At night if you listen, you can still
hear the river insisting on passage
Take you and me:
we join and join
Both of us tributaries of heritage
that brought us to this place
Our bodies carry memories within us
of our respective rivers
Too old to create new life,

I still make a new life from the old
We stand on the bank
and cast our prayers into the water
in tribute to those whose prayers
were silenced in their original languages
The language of the river transcends
miscommunication
The dam was in the English of the colonizer,
but the river is Indigenous,
sinuous, ingenious
Always flowing and joining,
expanding arteries of lifeblood,
despite the manmade flood

EAGLE BLESSING

All these birds on their way
Stopping point
Poised in water
Skeins in air
Gulls far from the sea
Pelicans awkwardly elegant
As a child, I dreamt I could fly
I would wake and feel disappointed
that I'd lost that power
Once, I ran from the top
of a hill, hoping to hoist
myself into the air
I stopped short, winded,
watching hawks' effortless
tilt and turn
Here I saw an eagle
busy over prey
then its lift off
all muscle and majesty
I instinctively lifted a prayer
as it arose in glorious expanse
Other birds are on their way,
migrating elsewhere,
while Eagle remains,
blessing this land
with thrust of wings
with feathers that adorn
your eagle staff
with the fearsome flight
of a survivor
of a warrior

Reservoir

There are things and memories
kept, set apart, bundled in story
This artificial lake contains
towns contains sorrows
contains first kisses,
birth, and death
When the dam was built
we were forced to move to higher ground
but memories were left below
and below the water, also
There are some who have seen
strange things on this water,
black-finned creature
shot at and missed
Bubbles of air from the dying
eventually stilled
Boats forge the surface
Sailboats regal in regatta
while the spirits of canoes
slip past, unnoticed
Thunderclouds appear
dark and menacing
You set someone on the hill
for fasting and prayer
One man stands and parts the storm
that was fast approaching in the sky
so that sun remains on sacred gathering
We keep what has always been ours
We reserve that right at least,

despite all taken and broken
despite all flooded,
there are still things and memories
kept, set apart, bundled in story

IMMERSION

You say you are beginning
to understand my texts in Cherokee,
what little I know:
Gvgeyu sgwisda nigohilv
Osd hitlvna
or the quick *hawa*
I miss the immersion
of the language class I took,
the sense of being steeped
in a deeper source and when,
maddeningly, all my German
came flooding back, unbidden,
from *that* immersion experience
in Germany, then Vermont
We say we'll both take an immersion
course in your language
You've already taught me a little;
I strive to pronounce it,
each syllable a struggle
Words river through us,
carrying different heritages—
you've got some French
I have some Deutsch—
As we stand by the lake
formed from force to river,
syllables swim in the water
and flow together,
finally emerging to rest on the bank
dried by the sun into imagined forms

Once, both our languages were forbidden
Every time we speak even a syllable
of our language
we express resistance

THESE RIVERS DO NOT MEET

except through tributary
of memory
Once, someone said to me,
"I don't know this river,"
when advising me on ceremony,
as if a river were a person,
which it is, in its rivering way,
more than I am,
with all my shifts and changes
Things suddenly flooded
or dammed up or dried up
to barely a trickle
I can still see light
refracting off the Oconaluftee
Drums from pow wow grounds
in time with the pound of my heart
I watched fish hoisted
blood and fish heads in the water
then roasted,
taking a bite, even though I don't eat meat anymore
The taste of chicory coffee
Jeep churning up dust
music blaring
Argument then long-held rupture before thaw
Scent of wild grapes on the walk along the river
to the restaurant, laughter under strung lights
Finally not feeling like a tourist
Now I cross rivers unknown to me,
not sites of Cherokee victory
Whereas the New snakes through
my mind, where my son and I canoed
while our dog stood guard

RIVERING

Rivering: in printing, creating streaks of white space in text caused by spaces between the words in several lines falling below each other

We	will	always	be	here
ev	enif	youcre	ate	supe
er	ficia	llakes	fro	mor
ig	inal	depth	Weg	ave
li	feto	ourp	eop	leWe
gi	veit	still		

UNRIVERED

The new news
brings back the old
All the blood in Alabama
emergency room
when ultrasound showed
no cardiac activity
The doctor saying I
wouldn't feel or remember
Hearing my own screams
from far away
The blood that unrivered
me for weeks and weeks
All the subsequent surgeries
I sometimes think it
would have been a daughter
I sometimes think my son
would have had a sister
Now that I am old
there is no flow
there is no moon time
Wounds do not
always heal
Not everything can
be cut out
At the river
in Cherokee I dipped
my son's stickball sticks
in the water
I saw blood in the water

from fish my then-friend caught
I do not know these rivers
I do not know the pain
of the earth's body
I just know that in that
Alabama emergency room
I was subject to removal
of that loss of life
and it pains me still

Deep Field

I learn to recognize
bright yellow of canola
Sahnish corn tassles early
Yucca thrusts white bloom
on the side of a hill
Someone tells me flax
blooms vivid blue
Field on field
and in between,
grasslands' undulation
that a friend takes a video of,
delighting in green dancing
I say it looks like waves
You tell me that's where
settlers got the name *prairie
schooner* for their wagons,
as grass resembled water
Then I see photos
from the Webb telescope
and learn that stars
are our relatives
and that light
takes longer than many
generations to reach us,
My class assignment
is to write a six word
story
I write: dying, I am
greeted by ancestors

SHELTERBELT

We lie warm and sated
like the animals we are
I stick to subjunctive,
speculate *if* about our future
You correct me with *when*
In this way
we begin to build
a life together
Subjunctive: contrary to fact,
my favorite mood when
I was learning German
I don't know enough Cherokee
to be at ease
Now I'm learning Sahnish
I wonder what the word is for *if*
I wonder what the word is for *when*
I wonder that this differentiation
is even possible
after all that's in the past
A storm comes up early morning,
but passes by the time
we venture out into the day,
sheltered by blue skies
Before I moved here
I'd never heard of shelterbelts,
stands of trees planted in a row
as a windbreak, offering reprieve
We are creating our own shelterbelt,
investing in protection for what we never

thought we'd have
Together we look at maps of where
the river used to run
We say the names of towns that are no more
We call and haul up shared but different
memories of flood, from which there was
no shelter

CEDAR CHEST

Cedar is sacred both to the Arikara and Cherokee,
as well as other tribes

We find it at an antiques store
(each of us having wanted one forever)

We haul it up to my apartment,
knowing one day it will grace our own place

We fill it with blankets and star quilts,
storing up warmth against the cold

I open it often, alone, and marvel at what my life holds

IRONHORSE

"Kill every buffalo you can!
Every buffalo dead is an Indian gone."

At the railroad museum
we board the caboose
that really is red
The word comes from words
meaning *a ship's cabin*
You climb into a seat,
pick up the phone
and suddenly the train
begins to move
We are on rails
to where the train
used to go,
to times that we've heard of
and read about,
but never seen
One high-up chair faces one way,
one the other
Past and future
ride the same rails—
looking forward,
looking back
Neither of us is astonished
by this impromptu and imagined journey
past field on field
of rippling grass,
of bison grazing,
wolves packing,
meadowlarks singing

It is winter and up ahead,
a special car plows mounds of snow out of the way
It is summer and heat shimmers
corn's silken tassels
When we pull back in to our starting station,
we carry the image of so many bison
crossing that trains had to stop
and wait for hours or even days for them to pass
This was before
the piles
of bison skulls
that passed
for progress

Night Ride

The hooked rug horses
bolt from their field of wool
and charge around the room at ceiling height,
their hooves pounding the walls,
gouging marks in plaster
(the rare earthquake in Maryland, your
dog's early warning, trying to herd you out
of the house as walls began to shake;
you thought it was you and that
you were having some kind of seizure.
Later, crack squiggled down
the wall of old home, marriage
crumbing on its foundation,
water starting to stain then pour and destroy
what had once been stable)
You remember your pony in her stable,
leading her to drink from mountain spring,
but these horse are wild, unbridled
You feel the wind as they pass over your head,
gaining speed as they gallop
Your own ponytail waves in the wake
of their movement
You stand and reaching, manage to grab a mane,
hoist yourself onto one of them,
and ride bareback as they burst in a herd
through the back screen door,
rising and riding into indigo sky
where stars are harmless spurs

17 SOUNDS

is what the book
says Arikara has
Apparently, if you
learn those sounds,
you can pronounce
any word, even if
you don't understand it
You say I talk too fast,
that Sahnish is meant
to be spoken slowly
and rather softly
I say that Cherokee
is best spoken if you
don't move your lips
You say I'll become
fluent before you do
I say I doubt it, since you
heard and learned it as a boy
and that the sounds will come
back to you; whereas
linguistic fossilization
occurs after around age 11
and then you'll always have
an accent
The river speaks its own language
Even under thick ice,
there is still flow
I remember a friend forbidden
from speaking his language

at boarding school, who later
was the elder in my immersion
class for learning Cherokee
Words survived and survive still
in flow of blood
Language, like the river,
can never truly be stopped,
as long as elders speak it
and as long as younger
generations listen and learn
I work on pronouncing the 17
sounds and in doing so,
our languages join
with English, the colonizer's
language, our common
knowledge
We will use it, bend it
to our purpose
like the river bends
around its banks
We will use it
to help the People,
sound by defiant sound

SUMMER SNOW

You send me pictures
from the grounds
outside your office
How cottonwood
tufts have covered
the ground like snow
One photo shows
your tracks in it
This constant
disorientation
of what looks
like something else
Like the flare I saw
shaped like a forked tongue
Like the lake
that looks placid
yet holds death
beneath
the surface

WASHINGTON

Native Americans serve in the armed forces at a higher
rate than any other demographic. No matter the conflict,
American Indian men and women continue to risk their lives
for the very government that practiced genocide and cultural
genocide against them

While you're at a veterans event
and send photos on your phone,
I remember Washington,
flying into National (never Reagan) airport
as unaccompanied minor, with my sister
Summers as traded children of divorce
The Smithsonian castle and monuments
The model of the blue whale a wonder
You send a photo of you in headdress,
by the Reflecting Pool
I remember Lafayette Square
with other poets, Secret Service threatening,
despite permit to protest
Reading at Busboys and Poets,
at the Indian museum
Taking the Metro, connecting the lines
my son memorized as a child
Pentagon smoking the day after
Terror of the snipers
My ex's lovers scattered over the city,
Jennifer in Dupont Circle,
the housekeeper at another office,
who was fired for *his* indiscretion
while I tried to hold things together

The Potomac in winter with thin ice,
where plane once crashed,
instilling fear of flying
Here, water freezes solid
Ice houses for fishing
Washington, where I met
a friend I still treasure
and former friend who breached trust
Washington of broken treaties
Washington of lies and promise
Washington, Town Destroyer
Washington, where my son, as a child,
carried in his father's arms,
reached up for cherry blossoms
falling like snow does
here on the Plains

ANTIETAM

"Antietam" is thought to derive from the
Algonquian for 'swift-flowing stream'

No sign of bloody battle
Just creek and sycamore
left as witness
I watch as you and my sister walk
down to the bridge
then turn to face me
for a photograph
Legions of dead
inhabit these fields
This creek tributary
to Potomac,
itself tributary
to Chesapeake Bay,
largest estuary,
tidal mouth,
as if bodies of water
had human body parts
At Antietam,
amputation was rampant
for survivors
My own body
compromised by covid's
original variant
Lungs and heart
fed by bloodstream
also diminished
Everyone fighting
hard and inward battles

as ghost tree shadows
late summer
after dropping helicopters
that dizzied to traumatized ground

HARPERS FERRY

Potomac and Shenandoah
merging together
Water green and cool
in summer heat
From the old railroad trestle
tables of rocks below in the river
Light-skinned innertubers
and kayakers paid to float
at leisure with their alcohol
Brown-skinned family
doused themselves freely,
diving and emerging
until a boy stood on a rock
with a woman who might
have been his mother,
both smiling for a photo
We sat and watched from the bank
as the memory of my son as a boy
along with his dog
drifted past, carried downstream
on the two mingled rivers
Hawks traced the sky
scouting for prey
Armory long-closed
Civil War supposedly over,
while rivers of blood still
fill and flood these national banks

HOLSTON

By the river there we sat down and wept
Driving into Knoxville,
the Holston a green mirror
where history is reflected
onto the present
On the trees there we hung up our harps
Confluence with French Broad
creates the Tennessee
First called the Cherokee River
by French explorers after encountered tribe
For our captors there required of us songs
British colonists renamed it for a settler
Rivers colonized by dams still retain their power
Treaty of the Holston broken,
as treaties mostly were
and our tormentors demanded of us mirth

NEW RIVER GORGE

Down into the gorge
with no cell service
River an old friend waiting
for reunion
Memories of canoeing
on this northward-flowing body
when your son was young
and found cobalt river glass,
shard of sky
unlike the bullet in the jar
removed from toddler
yellow fat still attached
Held high by doctor
for inspection by detective
Wail of mother
You keep bringing warm blankets,
warm blankets,
their small weight a comfort
during hours waiting for surgery,
survival uncertain
Later you pass through pathology
on the way to the morgue
and see jars of specimens
in reek of formaldehyde,
You choke on your own gorge
remembering specimens in museums,
body parts not repatriated,
bodies unreturned to the lands
and waters of home

CURRENT SEVERE ALERTS

This morning:
Dense Fog Advisory
Window packed with cotton
Impossible to see
Reminds me of Germany,
of North Carolina,
of the place in North Georgia
where the great frog
of Cherokee lore
squatted in wait
My first winter
you ensured I had
survival kit in my car
for threat of killing cold
White out from fog,
from snow
The weather and road
apps on my phone
my lifeline
Where am I starting from?
Where am I going?
Checking conditions
You say you've seen
tornadoes hurtling across the Plains
You say you can gauge
whether to keep driving
or to pull over
You tell me about
straight line winds

that do as much damage

as twisters

This being always on alert

suits my hypervigilance

Fog begins to lift

Cotton unpacking

like changing a dressing

The time in summer

we walked along a trail

snowy with cottonwood fluff

I picked a tuft up and it felt like cotton from back East

and I remembered my then-young son

wanting to stop and pick some

and my telling him the history

of slaves forced to pick cotton

just as people were forced onto the Trail,

forced off fertile land

All of us subject

to severe alerts,

even those who

know how to prepare

Some will always eschew safety

Some will always ensure calamity

The Opposite of Icthus

We are not a profile of defiling religion
We are not a symbol
We are real
We have been here a long time,
longer than the men with machines
and picks and loud discourse
that we feel underwater
as echo of an ill intent
We decide to keep swimming
We don't want to be trapped
Some of us will offer ourselves to those
who need sustenance
Someone has to be willing to sacrifice
We feel the displacement
of water against our gills
We do not want to be caught
and separated from our school
in this lie
in this lake
in this lie of a lake
So we keep swimming
We let the river carry us
We shine silver and pewter
We keep swimming
We keep shining

SMUDGING

You suggest we smudge the rental camper
before settling in, as well as ourselves
to clear negative energy and thoughts
after bad start to eagerly-awaited trip
This after my several-hour departure,
holding the wheel with one hand,
the other gripping the bar on the car door
to feel the pulse of the music in attempt
to get grounded
I ask you to keep your hand on my leg
to help me get back into my body
Doesn't everyone fly away at times?
Trick learned for survival:
hiding from threat by dissociation
Now in our camper the fragrant
smoke of sage and cedar and sweetgrass
We stand wreathed in present blessing
There will never be another now

Delta

It was time to slow down
after all that rushing
I put down sediment
after sediment,
until there was a bas(e)is
for myself
triangle of repose
This newly-formed land
is not a part of those who
eroded me, harnessed me
Bull sharks in fresh water
Unexpected threat
Flash and thrash of fin
Eventually I create this
new place from which
to view the flow
Accrual on accrual
I have all the world in the time

WATER CYCLE

This cycle continues
This replenishment
The opposite of trauma
that cycles to deplete,
generation after generation
We all need fresh water
and many don't receive it
On the Plains, clouds form and turn
You tell me you can see tornadoes coming
I say that is of little comfort
We cycle through grief
yet are fed by its springs

IN WHICH YOU SAY YOU LOVE ME IN YOUR LANGUAGE

Before heading opposite directions
on the highway we pull into a park
at night where canopy of stars is so
real it looks fake. Suddenly we are on a set
Cue holding me close Cue pan of stars wheeling
and blazing like flares on the Bakken
Cue coyotes (we pronounce this differently)
yipping then howling, coming in so close
I ask if we need to be worried
You say they've had enough to eat and that it's
only in times of starvation we would
need to be concerned. They're so close I expect
to be able to see their eyes like in Knoxville
when I took out the trash with my dog
and the coyotes ranged close, with flashing eyes
Cue: your lips on my mouth, my neck. My hands
freeing your hair from its ponytail holder
Me clasping you close. Cue wind in the trees,
add the perfect amount of rustling sound
Slash of passing headlights illuminates your face
You are leaving to visit relatives
in Nebraska. There you'll learn how to say "I
love you" in your language. You'll first text, then say it
We'd been using English or my Cherokee
Now we have three ways to say it, but I
like my way best: gvgeyu, I am stingy with you
I pronounce your way slowly, catching on
the different s's, the silent A at the end
You tell me you've never said I love you
to anyone in your language before
I am stilled in awe by this significance
We add this to our growing list of firsts

BLUE HOLE SPRING

Its blue sheen a bowl of calm
Source of spring, healing balm

This water wells with dreams,
eddies with memories that stream

past, reflecting Cherokee
gathered in Council at Red Clay

Like me, they came seeking solace
and wisdom at this hallowed place

that is timeless as our
Eternal Flame, ardent every hour

Removal did not smother
fire of People, strong together

From limestone ledge, this pool
from the underworld unspools,

pouring forth its watersong,
trilling along over stones

I go to water with uncried tears
offered in sacrifice for years

of loss—mine, and generations
Water is rejuvenation

I stand with the current,
clear and cool, giving respite

Leaf loosens, lazes onto surface,
conjures concentric circles

Timeless water and mountains
contrast with my own decline

On a day far from home
I will see white clouds foam

around blue pool of sky
and will wonder why,

when hearts still yearn
and desire yet burns,

I can feel so alone
while Blue Hole Spring blues on

Blue Hole Spring, translated into Cherokee by Barbara Duncan

Degalawi'v Amogiwa

ᏕᎦᎳᏫ'Ꭵ ᎠᎼᎩᏩ

Its blue sheen a bowl of calm
Source of spring, healing balm

Sakonige'i atalugisgo'i, iyusdi unvweda, tohi
Nvwoti ganugogv'i
ᏌᎪᏂᎨ'Ꭲ ᎠᏔᎷᎩᏍᎪ'Ꭲ, ᎢᏳᏍᏗ ᎤᏅᏪᏓ, ᏙᎯ
ᏅᏬᏘ ᎦᏄᎪᎬ'Ꭲ

This water wells with dreams,
eddies with memories that stream

Ama asgitsv'vsgo'i
ama unvdaha, ama ageyo'i.
ᎠᎹ ᎠᏍᎩᏨ'ᎥᏍᎪ'Ꭲ
ᎠᎹ ᎤᏅᏓᎭ, ᎠᎹ ᎠᎨᏲ'Ꭲ.

past, reflecting Cherokee
gathered in Council at Red Clay

Ani-Tsalagi ama atalugi'a
Ela-Wodiyi danadlosgv'i
ᎠᏂ-ᏣᎳᎩ ᎠᎹ ᎠᏔᎷᎩ'Ꭰ
ᎡᎳ-ᏬᏗᏱ ᏓᎾᏝᏍᎬ'Ꭲ

Like me, they came seeking solace
and wisdom at this hallowed place

Aya iyusdi, gatiyo dogilutsv'i
hani, tohi nole aktasdi digihyohv'i
ᎠᏯ ᎢᎠ᎐ᎠᏗ, ᏍᏗᎯ ᏞᏯᎷᏣ᎐ᏛᏔ
ᎭᏂ, ᏞᎫ ᏃᎹ ᎠᏍᏚᎢᏗ ᏞᎧᏂᏩᏔ

that is timeless as our
Eternal Flame, ardent every hour

"Igatlosgi Nigesvna Adawelagisgi" iyusdi
Nigohila utlinigida, nigohila usgasidi
"ᏔᏍᎫᎢᏅᎩ ᎲᏝᏒᎠ ᎠᏞᏍᎫᏩᏯᎢᏅ" ᎠᎬᏗ
ᎭᏞᎫᏪ ᎤᏣᎲᏌᏢ, ᎭᏞᎫᏪ ᎤᎧᎠᏍᏲᎠ

Removal did not smother
fire of People, strong together

Tsige'vgvwotana'i gesdi yi dugasvstanvhi
atsila Ani-Tsalagi unitseli, degadoga unitlinigida
ᎲᏝᎢᎴᎥᏬᎠᏔ ᏫᎢᎠᎠ Ꮴ ᏍᏍᏒᎥᏯᎤᏙᎫ
ᎠᎲᏔ ᎠᎲᎦᎾᎩ ᎤᎯᏤᏈ, ᏍᏍᏞᏍ ᎤᎲᏣᎲᏢ

From limestone ledge, this pool
from the underworld unspools,

Gosda uneganvya ama ganugogo'i
ama ageyo'i elohi hawini
ᎠᎥᏢ ᎤᎾᎢᏍᎤᎥᎧ ᎠᎪ ᏍᎦᎠᎠᏔ
ᎠᎪ ᎠᎲᎯᏔ ᎡᎦᎠ ᎭᏮᎭ

pouring forth its watersong,
trilling along over stones

ama atsv'vsga, ama dekanogi'a
galvladitsa nvya, gega, dekanogi'a
ᎠᎹ ᎠᏨ'ᎥᏍᎦ, ᎠᎹ ᏕᎧᏃᎩ'Ꭰ
ᎦᎸᎳᏗᏣ ᏅᏯ, ᎨᎦ, ᏕᎧᏃᎩ'Ꭰ

I go to water with uncried tears
offered in sacrifice for years

Amayi gego'i tsutsohyisdi gesdi yigatsoyiha
tsudetiyvda gagwiyiha
ᎠᎹᏱ ᎨᎪ'Ꭲ ᏧᏦᏱᏍᏗ ᎨᏍᏗ ᏱᎦᏦᏱᎭ
ᏧᏕᏘᏴᏓ ᎦᏇᏱᎭ

of loss—mine, and generations
Water is rejuvenation

tsunanelotanvsv, ogiyohuselv'i
ama atse nigvneho'i
ᏧᎾᏁᎶᏔᏅᏒ, ᎣᎩᏲᎱᏎᎸ'Ꭲ
ᎠᎹ ᎠᏤ ᏂᎬᏁᎰ'Ꭲ

I stand with the current,
clear and cool, giving respite

Amayi ageyo'i tsiyadogo'i
ulvsati nole unesahyvdla, ama agwadawesolvsdiha
ᎠᎹᏱ ᎠᎨᏲ'Ꭲ ᏥᏯᏙᎪ'Ꭲ
ᎤᎸᏌᏘ ᏃᎴ ᎤᏁᏌᏴᏜ, ᎠᎹ ᎠᏆᏓᏪᏐᎸᏍᏗᎭ

Leaf loosens, lazes onto surface,
conjures concentric circles

Ugaloga ahida galosga
gasagwala adahnesagi'a
ᎤᎦᎶᎦ ᎠᎯᏓ ᎦᎶᏍᎦ
ᎦᏌᏆᎳ ᎠᏓᏁᏌᎩ'Ꭰ

Timeless water and mountains
contrast with my own decline

Nigohila ama, nigohila dunvdasvhi, hani danedoli
Aseno agwatsvgo'i, kedali gega, datsiyo'osi
ᏂᎪᎯᎳ ᎠᎹ, ᏂᎪᎯᎳ ᏚᏅᏓᏒᎯ, ᎭᏂ ᏓᏁᏙᎵ
ᎠᏎᏃ ᎠᏆᏨᎪ'Ꭲ, ᎨᏓᎵ ᎨᎦ, ᏓᏥᏲ'ᎣᏏ

On a day far from home
I will see white clouds foam

Sogwo iga, dagwenvsv inage'i
Unega ulogila, unilogisgesdi detsiwonihi
ᏐᏉ ᎢᎦ, ᏓᏇᏅᏒ ᎢᎾᎨ'Ꭲ
ᎤᏁᎦ ᎤᎶᎩᎳ, ᎤᏂᎶᎩᏍᎨᏍᏗ ᏕᏥᏬᏂᎯ

around blue pool of sky
and will wonder why,

Tsulogila sakonige'i galvladi danadadeyvsdani
Gadono? Dagadanteli
ᏧᎶᎩᎳ ᏌᎪᏂᎨ'Ꭲ ᎦᎸᎳᏗ ᏓᎾᏓᏕᏴᏍᏓᏂ
ᎦᏙᏃ ᏓᎦᏓᏅᏖᎵ

when hearts still yearn
and desire yet burns,

Ogadando yuninigvgo'igwo
Ogadulisgi yadawelagisgo'i
ᏓᎦᏓᏅᎢ ᏢᏂᏂᎬᎪ'ᎢᎬᎳ
ᏓᎦᏍᏈᎣᎠᏫ ᏯᏓᏪᎳᎩᏍᎪᎠ'Ꭲ

I can feel so alone
while Blue Hole Spring blues on

Gadono agwasv agwadanvta
Sakonige Yamogwa, nigohila sakonige'igwo.
ᎦᏙᏃ ᎠᏆᏒ ᎠᏆᏓᏅᏔ
ᏌᎪᏂᎨ ᏯᎼᏆ, ᏂᎪᎯᎳ ᏌᎪᏂᎨ'ᎢᎬᎣ.

Look,

I don't know what to tell you
I can't (although I could) lie
and tell you things will get easier
Or that you won't dream of the one
who hurt you the most,
waking to uncertainty,
since dream-touch is so real
Those towns don't stop being towns
even underwater
Memories submerged still move
There's still that one picture
you can't fathom:
how trusting you were
how stupidly happy
Look at your face—
that openness
that smile
from being beguiled
You go back and gather yourself into your arms
and shush all the crying from regret
No point in that
Kiss your new, true lover
Get up
Scrape the drapes wide
Today you will go to the river

Notes:

Garrison Dam and Tellico Dam: The construction of the Garrison Dam, begun in 1947 and completed in 1953, flooded ancestral homelands, including over 90% of fertile river valley land, of the Arikara, Mandan, and Hidatsa, forcing communities onto more barren high ground, despite protest from the tribes and violation of former treaty. The dam resulted in forcible relocation of approximately 80% of MHA Nation's tribal membership at the time. Council Chairman George Gillette in a tearful forced "consent" to the coercive piece of legislation, stated, "The truth is, as everyone knows, our Treaty of Fort Laramie...and our constitution are being torn to shreds by this contract." A recent United Thank Offering grant in environmental reparations is a step towards acknowledging the damage wrought by the resulting flood. The dam created the third largest reservoir in the United States, Lake Sakakawea. Submerged Native American towns include Sanish, Elbowoods, and Nishu.

Similarly, in the Southeast, the Tellico Dam built by the Tennessee Valley Authority flooded Cherokee towns and sacred sites, despite protest from the Cherokee. From an historical marker: "After 18 years of protests from farmers, Native Americans, and environmentalists...TVA completed Tellico Dam in 1980, thereby flooding Overhill Cherokee village sites such as the sacred town, Chota." The dam also flooded the sites of Tanasi (from which "Tennessee" is derived), Toqua, Tomotley, Citico, Mialoquo, and Tuskegee. In 1979, three Cherokee individuals and two Cherokee bands filed a lawsuit against the Tennessee Valley Authority (TVA) to prevent the flooding. The lawsuit was unsuccessful. The construction of both the Garrison Dam in North Dakota and the Tellico Dam in Tennessee demonstrated callous disregard for Native land and People.

Blue Hole Spring: Located in what is now Red Clay State Historic Park in Cleveland, Tennessee, site of the last seat of Cherokee government before the 1838 enforcement of the Indian Removal Act of 1830 by the U.S. military, which resulted in the forced removal of Cherokee people from their homelands on what is known as The Trail of Tears, when thousands died from disease, starvation, and exposure. Blue Hole Spring was the source of water for the Councils of 1832-1837. The Cherokee believe that the streams which come from mountains are the trails by which we reach the underworld and the springs at their heads are the doorways by which we enter it, but to do this one must fast and go to water and have one of the underworld people for a guide.

Cherokee translator of "Blue Hole Spring": BARBARA R. DUNCAN worked for twenty-three years as Education Director at the Museum of the Cherokee Indian, taught Cherokee language at University of North Carolina Asheville, and is the author of award-winning books on Cherokee history, culture, and folklore. She has also collaborated to write a curriculum for Cherokee language in four textbooks and a website. She is retired and lives in the mountains of western North Carolina.

Of mixed descent, including Cherokee, KIMBERLY L. BECKER's other poetry collections are *Words Facing East* and *The Dividings* (WordTech Editions), *The Bed Book* and *Bringing Back the Fire* (Spuyten Duyvil), and *Flight* (MadHat Press). Poetry Daily featured "Rivering," the title poem from this sixth book. Her seventh book, *Uktena: A Poetic Narrative*, based on a traditional Cherokee story, is forthcoming from MadHat Press. Her work appears widely, including *Indigenous Message on Water, Women Write Resistance: Poets Resist Gender Violence, Tending the Fire: Native Voices and Portraits, Unpapered: Writers Consider Native American Identity and Cultural Belonging*, and *23 Tales: Appalachian Ghost Stories, Legends, and Other Mysteries*.

kimberlylbecker.com

www.ingramcontent.com/pod-product-compliance
Lightning Source LLC
Chambersburg PA
CBHW031246120626
46545CB00007B/2666